SEX AND THE SINGLE PANDA

SEX AND THE SINGLE PANDA

The Revolting Pursuit of Love in the Animal Kingdom

by Dahlia Gallin Ramirez

CHRONICLE BOOKS
SAN FRANCISCO

Library of Congress Cataloging-in-Publication Data is available.

ISBN: 978-1-7972-1399-6

Manufactured in China.

Design by Jon Glick.

10 9 8 7 6 5 4 3 2 1

Chronicle Books LLC
680 Second Street
San Francisco, CA 94107
www.chroniclebooks.com

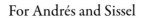

For Andrés and Sissel

INTRODUCTION

The idea for this book came while I was watching a nature special about rabbits. No spoilers (because it's in this book), but their courtship ritual is nuts. I started thinking about how rabbits, and other creatures, might describe their own mating behavior—a sort of dating profile but with the raw honesty that animals do best.

I started with the obvious bad boys—the exploding genitalia, the spraying feces—and then delved into the subtler waters of fake DILFs, leg-wrestlers, and balloon artists. And then the females, God help us. While they may be harder to spot, they make up for it in sheer, vile terror.

When it comes to seeking a mate, animals are just like people you might know: proud, aggressive, earnest, deceptive, heartbreakingly vulnerable, and—mostly—very, very horny.

You may see yourself in here. Or maybe you'll recognize an ex. You may find yourself saying things like, "I would have sex with the clownfish!" Don't worry, it's not bestiality; it's just an innocent thought experiment, and we all do it. I, for one, have a crush on the southern ground hornbill.

Speaking of raw honesty, many people have read details in this book and asked, "Is that really true?" Yes, everything in this book is true. The only things that aren't entirely scientifically accurate are the eyes and eyebrows that I drew on some of the animals, especially the spiders. I just had to give them some personality, because honestly, I can't even tell which end is the "face."

And finally, a word of caution followed by a word of wisdom: Almost everything in this book is what you might call "disgusting." I'll ask you to remember that everything depicted here is 100% from nature, and nature can never be wrong.

BACHELOR

I will present you with a beautiful, silk-wrapped gift.
It may be a tasty treat, the corpse of a competitor, a twig, or—
psych!—nothing at all. While you unwrap it, I'll mate with
you, hopefully finishing before you realize it's the latter.

Want the gift but not me? I'll just play dead, clutching
the gift in my stiff, cold hands. As you drag the gift away,
I'll dingleberry along with it. When you get me home, I'll
magically revive and chase you around the kitchen table. If
you're not a little bit in love with me by then, you're nuts.

I am a

NURSERY WEB SPIDER

Pisaura mirabilis

Many animals play dead to avoid being eaten, but male nursery web spiders are the only known pervs who play dead to get laid. This behavior is called "thanatosis," and it's charming enough to work on its own. But throw a fake nuptial gift into the mix? Too naughty; we'll take it!

BACHELORETTE

If you want to be with me, you need to be 100 percent okay with the fact that I can take down a wildebeest by myself, I can chew bones to a fine powder, and my penis is bigger than yours. You heard me right: I have a "pseudo penis" and "pseudo scrotum," but there's nothing pseudo about having to roll my ween back like a tube sock for sex. And when it's time to give birth, let me just say this: Imagine giving birth through your dong. Now watch me do it.

I am a

SPOTTED HYENA

Crocuta crocuta

Relax your mind, and prepare for a confusing anatomy lesson.
The pseudo scrotum is actually fused-shut vaginal labia. And
the pseudo penis is a seven-inch clitoris with an opening
for urination (okay), sex (oy), and childbirth (omfg).

BACHELOR

I know you ladies are in the mood only eight to twelve hours a year, so I won't waste your time. I'll climb up a tree, about seven feet above you, and drench you with urine. If you appreciate that, we'll mate. If you don't, I'm in major fucking trouble.

I am a

PORCUPINE

Erethizon dorsatum

Yes, female North American porcupines really are fertile only once a year, every September, for a window of eight to twelve hours. The rest of the year, they are so sexually inactive that the vagina is *literally* closed for business, sealed over with a membrane. If the female likes the guy, the super-soaking stimulates her to go into estrus. If not, she screams at him, shakes herself off, and runs away.

URINE

Peepee. There's a reason it's called "number one." This liquid calling card tells potential partners a lot about you, including the fact that "you're in" to "urine." Let's meet some elite members of the Urinati.

LOBSTER

To coax her way into a hunk's den, a female lobster wafts urine into his home, essentially drugging him with her wizz. Intoxicated, he has no choice but to invite her in.

GIRAFFE

You know how a restaurant server pours you a little bit of wine and then stands there awkwardly while you taste it and say it's fine? In giraffe land, that's called "the Flehmen sequence," and instead of wine, it's piss. The female offers a taste test to the male. If it has an ovulatory bouquet, it's on.

BACHELORETTE

I'll save you a few boring dinners by telling you that I don't do sex. My kind is all-female, all day long, and we populate without the copulate. That's right; no men. It's like Wonder Woman's all-girl island, Themyscira, only if Chris Pine washed up on the beach we'd let him rot like a whale. My idea of a perfect date is pound cake followed by tweezing my eyebrows. But I have to be careful, because the last time I looked in the mirror too long I got pregnant.

I am a

NEW MEXICO WHIPTAIL LIZARD

Cnemidophorus neomexicanus

Long ago, a renegade (or poor-sighted) female ancestor of this lizard mated with a lizard from another species and gave her daughter a payload of double chromosomes. So now these whiptails can make selfie babies ad infinitum, without ending up like the Hapsburgs.

BACHELOR

I like a woman who's bigger than me. If you choose me, and if something tragic should ever happen to you, I will turn female, take your place, and have my pick of male suitors. (Definitely going for Brian.) Then I'll finally understand all your complicated emotions, but it will be too late because you'll be dead.

I am a

CLOWNFISH

Amphiprioninae

Clownfish—sequential hermaphrodites—are all born male, but one can turn female if he's very, very lucky. One dominant female rules a group of males, along with her boy toy of choice. If she dies, he gets to grief eat until he basically becomes her.

BACHELORETTE

I'm sexy, I'm independent, and there's a 13 to 28 percent chance I'll gnaw your head off during sex—and not because I'm horrible or depraved. Because I'm hungry. And you're there. I know "sexual cannibal" looks bad on paper, but sex isn't bad, and neither is cannibalism, so I don't get why it's *soooo horrible* when they happen together. (And anyway, you'll like the sex better without that dumb head-brain.)

I am a

PRAYING MANTIS

Mantodea

The male can indeed continue copulating—walking around, even—
without his head. (Don't ever watch this. You'll throw up and cry.)
Females that chomp heads lay more and healthier eggs, which means
they're not being gross; they're just being really good mommies.

HOW TO LIVE WITH A SEXUAL CANNIBAL

She's beautiful, she's twice your size, she's a sexual cannibal . . . and you love her. Here's how to optimize survival with this very special lady.

SOMETIMES YOUR HEAD LOOKS YUMMY

I love you but I don't trust you

Feed her. Often and much. A well-fed sexual cannibal is likely to be harmless for at least an hour. In fact, a huge meal before intimacy can be a wonderful, sexy tradition.

NACHOS.
NACHOS!
NACHOS!!!

Have a safe word. It will build trust in your relationship and give you both confidence—and that's the foundation for a strong, intimate connection.

Open, positive communication is key for every relationship. When tensions arise, use "I" statements to focus on your feelings. Because when a sexual cannibal feels judged or cornered, she may get snacky.

SOMETIMES I FEEL UNSAFE WHEN YOU STARE AT ME DURING LOVEMAKING.

"I" statements not cutting it? Pretend to be female—fast. The "friend zone" is a very safe place to be with a sexual cannibal. And there's no reason why you can't have an honest conversation while pretending to be someone else.

And finally, a note to the cannibals: Learn to identify the difference between feeling horny and hungry. Do you want Mark Ruffalo or an everything bagel? If that question gives you pause, you're not alone. But eat something.

BACHELOR

No, that's not a small arm; it's a big penis. Okay, if you want to get technical about it, it *is* sort of an arm, but if it walks like a dick and talks like a dick and impregnates like a dick. . . . Did I mention it's detachable? Not as great as it sounds. My "arm" will explode out of me, finds its way over to you, and you get to keep it as a souvenir. Enjoy. Don't worry about me. I've had an okay life.

I am an

ARGONAUT OCTOPUS

Argonauta argo

The detachable penis? It's a specially adapted arm called a *hectocotylus*, used to deliver sperm to the female. She's 8 times larger and 600 times heavier than he is, so no wonder he needs to send an attaché detaché.

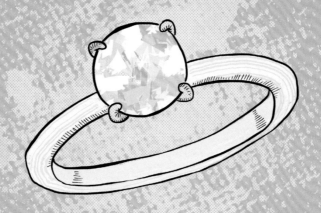

BACHELORETTE

All my girlfriends keep asking me, "When is Bill gonna put a rock on your finger!?!?" To which I say, "I don't know what you're talking about. What's a finger?" I *do* love rocks, though. Josh surprised Stacy with a brown rock in her tapioca on Valentine's Day in Times Square. And Jen got a gray rock dropped from a tiny parachute into her cleavage during a family reunion. But I don't need anything fancy like that. Just a rock, and I'll know Bill's The One!!!

I am an

ADÉLIE PENGUIN

Pygoscelis adeliae

"Say it with a pebble." Penguins do love a nice, shiny rock.
A courting male will scour the beach for just the right stone,
maybe even stealing a good one from a nearby nest. But
you just can't stay mad at those waddly little scamps.

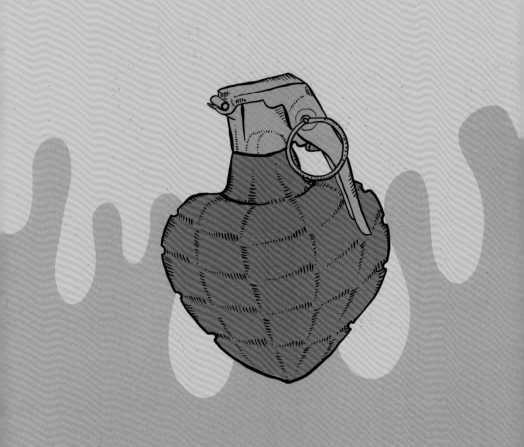

BACHELOR

As soon as we're done making love (also known as two seconds after starting), my balls will literally explode, killing me instantly. But my unscathed peen will block your tunnel from any competitor males. Winning!

I am a

WESTERN HONEY BEE

Apis mellifera

Winning for a little while, at least. What he (mercifully) doesn't know is that his "unscathed peen" actually reflects ultraviolet light, acting as a beacon to other horny, suicidal drones. Here are the grim mechanics: One by one, each male removes the previous guy's debris ("Hmm, what's that? Toss it."), copulates, and detonates—his life mission gloriously accomplished.

BALLOONS

Balloons aren't just for idiots. In fact, they are a sex magnet so effective that some animals have evolved a built-in clown show. Let's take a look at some of nature's original 'looners.

BALLOON FLY

A huge balloon to bat around during sex? That's a "Hell, yes." During breeding season, swarms of males gather to parade their "nuptial gifts"—delicate, white silk balloons.

HOODED SEAL

The male hooded seal blows out a colossal "nasal balloon" to attract ladies and terrify other males. Just like an angry, horny clown.

FRIGATEBIRD

The male with the biggest balloon gets the girl. Which is why—and this is heartbreaking—he gently covers your eyes with his wings during sex so that you don't see a guy with a better balloon.

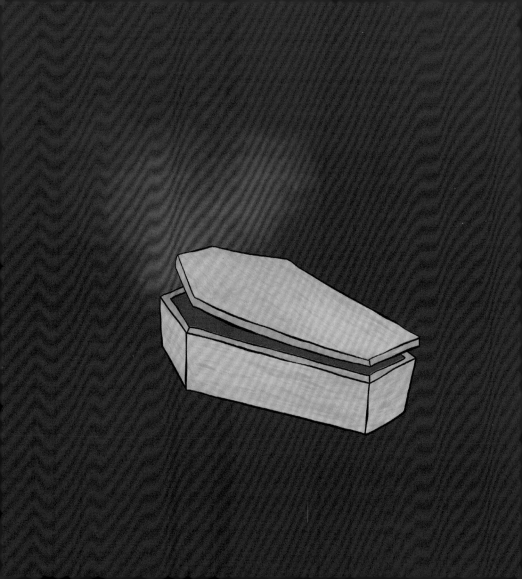

BACHELORETTE

I'm dead. Totally dead. And not just recently deceased, but actually starting to putrefy. I'll acknowledge that I'm not a dynamo in the sack and I don't blink much, but I'm severely offended. You're just going at it like, "Oh, I'm such a great lover," and I'm literally a corpse. Is this what I normally smell like to you? Can you roll off and let me rest in peace now?

I am a

TEGU LIZARD

Salvator merianae

The dead are a huge, untapped dating market, but several species of lizard have given it a go. One particular dead female tegu lizard was the hot girl at the dance for not one but two males who were observed mating with her. Female tegu lizards are quite torpid during sex, so— to be fair—the males may have thought it was pretty good for her.

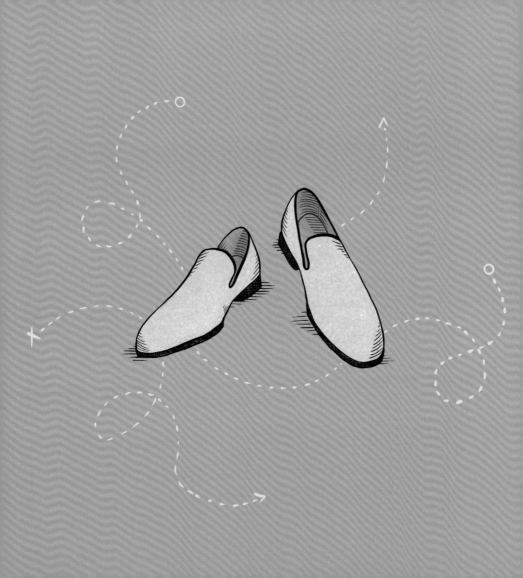

BACHELOR

Can you move back a little? Thanks. I am going to perform a dance that I inherited from my father, and his father before him. My great-great-grandfather invented the "double-reverse oh-no-you-didn't" that has been widely imitated (including by Sir David Attenborough, who sucked at it). Daddy has been training me for this dance my entire life, and he's kind of a bitch about it, so I really hope you like it.

I am a

BIRD OF PARADISE

Paradisaeidae

Having a tough-ass dance dad will only get you so far in this business. You need to be a quintuple threat with charisma coming out of every hole. And while you shape-shift and sing your guts out, a dull little female with the coloration and personality of a lunch bag looks on impassively, judging you.

DANCE

Everyone knows that if you're a good dancer, you're good at sex.
After all, you can move your arms and legs really well. And if
you're good at sex, you're probably good at making babies.

FLAMINGO

Clustered together like tourists in a sketchy part of town, the males parade for the females, head-whipping, wing-flashing, and showing off 134 (yes, really) dance moves that take decades to master.

PRAIRIE CHICKEN

Males congregate and dance for two months straight. Only one or two dominant males get 90 percent of the females, but they *all* attract middle-aged human birders, some from as far away as Canada!

SCORPION

The scorpion *Promenade à Deux* may look romantic, but here's what's really going on: pincers clasped, pushing against each other, she's testing his strength, and he's searching for a place to deposit his sperm packet.

61

BACHELORX

I'm male and female, which means I can do you, you can do me,
we can do we, and—in a pinch—me can do me. I've got a huge
penis, a basic vagina, and questionable problem-solving skills.
Sometimes a schlong gets stuck. And no spoilers, but have you
seen that movie about the rock climber who has to chew off
his own arm? That could be us, sex-wise. And if you chew off
mine, I'll probably chew off yours, too, just so we're even.

I am a

BANANA SLUG

Ariolimax dolichophallus

When a banana slug humblebrags to you that sex is challenging because of their enormous penis, don't roll your eyes. It's real. But do they really have to chew it off to get free? Of course not. *Nobody* does. Scientists have been watching this plantain horror show for ages, and they still aren't entirely sure why they do it. One theory? That love is a beautiful mystery.

BACHELORETTE

Excuse me for living, but I love a man who can sing. When I get backstage, I'm gonna deposit my larvae on your hot bod; they'll bore into your flesh, then tear their way out a week later, *Alien*-style. You'll be dead within seconds. Price you pay for those pipes, Boccelli.

I am a

PARASITIC FLY

Ormia ochracea

Not all groupies are equal. Loud male field crickets attract female field crickets . . . as well as eavesdropping parasitic flies. These crickets may be chirping themselves right out of the gene pool, making room for the quiet guys.

SONG

Guys with great pipes melt serious underwear. It's called "The Musician Effect." The thinking is that any male who has the spare time to write a love song must have covered his basic survival skills.

GREEN FROG

Females gauge the attractiveness of males by the sound of their voices in the dark. So clever little jerk frogs imitate the low-pitched voices of larger, more desirable mates.

HAMMERHEAD BAT

Bat girls love guys who can honk really, really loud. So the males are exquisitely designed for honking and not much else. If there were a chain of restaurants that objectified them, it would be called Honkers.

HUMPBACK WHALE

Males gather in large groups called "arenas" to sing their haunting mating song. If you play the song sped up, it's "The Gambler" by Kenny Rogers.

BACHELOR

I hope you enjoy our lovemaking, because when we're done, I'll spackle your vag closed. It's gonna be like the tomb of Tutankhamun in there. And as long as I've got the trowel out, I might as well cement the genitals of those other guys who are eyeing you. They're going to look like a bunch of Ken dolls when I'm done with them.

I am a

SPINY-HEADED WORM

Acanthocephalan

Spiny-headed worms are ingenious parasites that live in the gut wall of an unsuspecting host. (Don't worry, it's not you. It's a duck at best.) They are so highly adapted to the parasitic mode of life that they have lost all but their most essential organs. For the male, that's the proboscis, penis, balls, and—of course—the indispensable "cement gland" to seal the deal.

BACHELORETTE

Like my perfume? I know, I smell incredible. It's as if all the most beautiful, intelligent women in the world were fed pure vanilla, wrapped in Corinthian leather, sent to a free-trial hot yoga class, blended together, simmered to a reduction, and then sprayed all over me. I smell so sexy, I've had men follow me into crafting-supply stores. Seriously, it's a problem sometimes. But you, I like you . . . come a little closer. A little closer . . .

I am a

BOLAS SPIDER

Mastophoreae

The female bolas spider is an unassuming little lump who catfishes male moths by wafting out the scent of a gorgeous she-moth in heat. When he gets within whiffing range, she swings a lasso (with her goddamned *leg*), globs him with the sticky "bola" at the end of it, and reels him in for dinner. This olfactory con is called "aggressive chemical mimicry." Call it what you want—a girl's gotta eat.

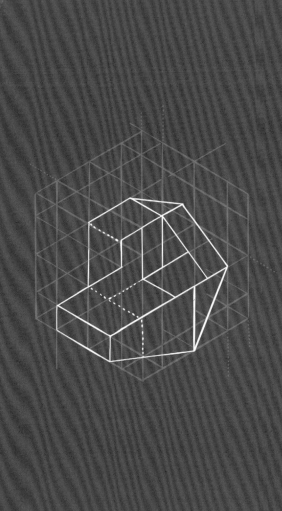

BACHELOR

Look. At. It. I've spent the last year perfecting this space, and it is absolutely superb. I guess I would call it an indoor-outdoor primitive pop-art Bauhaus constructivist monochromatic earthwork muff-magnet. I personally curated and anally arranged 600 found cerulean *objets* that serve a dual purpose of creating a thought space and drawing the eye right to my genitalia.

I am a

SATIN BOWERBIRD

Ptilonorhynchus violaceus

Bowerbirds are brilliant architects and artists, building stunning structures using everything at their disposal: flower petals, seeds, condom wrappers . . . But, like many great artists, they're also kind of assholey. They vandalize and steal from other males' bowers, and they get really pissy if you so much as *touch* one of their perfectly placed objects.

HOME DÉCOR

If the design vibe of your home is "safety from predators," that's a fantastic start. But you may want to take a note from these decorators, who elevate their spaces to truly copulatory levels.

PUFFER FISH

Bachelors build huge, geometric sand mandalas on the sea floor to attract a mate. Until recently, these were thought to be the work of aliens. But fish *are* kind of like aliens!

ROCK SPARROW

These nondescript little brown birds decorate their nests with the feathers of flashier birds. Just like having a poster of Marilyn Monroe in your room.

GIANT PACIFIC OCTOPUS

These solitary souls decorate their dens with shells and other crusty jewels of the sea. But it might not be for mating. Apparently, these big-brained creatures need a hobby or they get extremely depressed.

85

BACHELOR

God, you're beautiful. First chance I get, I'll sink my teeth into you, attach myself to you permanently, and live as a parasite on your body. I will eventually become absorbed into you, with only a pair of gonads remaining to remember the good times. You can use those 'nads whenever you feel like making babies. You're welcome!

I am an

ANGLER FISH

Melanocetus johnsonii

"To be driven by impelling odor headlong upon a mate so gigantic, in such immense and forbidding darkness, and willfully to eat a hole in her soft side, to feel the gradually increasing transfusion of her blood through one's veins, to lose everything that marked one as other than a worm, to become a brainless, senseless thing that was a fish . . ."

—Naturalist William Beebe, 1938

THAT'S ME!

BACHELORETTE

If you follow me around long enough, I will eventually turn around. And punch you in the face. Then you'd better jump straight up into the air—at least 15 feet, asshole—and flip 180 degrees while I run under you. Then I'll do the jump-and-spin while you run under me. We'll do this again and again and again, until I'm so bored I don't care who fathers my children.

I am a

COTTONTAIL RABBIT

Sylvilagus

Cottontail courtship behavior is called "cavorting," but don't be fooled by the adorable name. All that running, jumping, and face-punching can scatter chunks of hide and hair for acres. Like other violent courtship rituals, it weeds out the weak and the sane.

10 SURPRISING SIGNS SHE'S <u>INTO YOU</u>

OOPS, DID
I HIT YOU?

She throws rocks at you.
Hard. (*Capuchin monkey*)

PERFECT
NURSERY
SHITPILE!

She wants to raise your babies
on a pile of excrement. (*Fly*)

LET'S LIVE IN
THE MOMENT.

She kills you *after* copulating,
not before. (*Praying mantis*)

WANT TO WATCH
"STEEL MAGNOLIAS"
AGAIN?

Your tears turn her on.
(*Mouse*)

I LOVE BABIES.

She kills all your friends'
babies. (*Meerkat*)

CAN I HAVE A
FRY THANKS.

She steals your food.
(*Orangutan*)

MMM THAT
WAS NICE.

She's fine with you throwing up
in her mouth. (*Parrot*)

RIGHT HERE,
DUMMY.

She glows fluorescent green.
(*Shiny jumping spider*)

JUST LIKE THE
QUEEN DOES!

She walks toward you backward.
(*Japanese macaque*)

YOOOOOOOLK!!!

She lays an egg with a really
big yolk. (*Canary*)

95

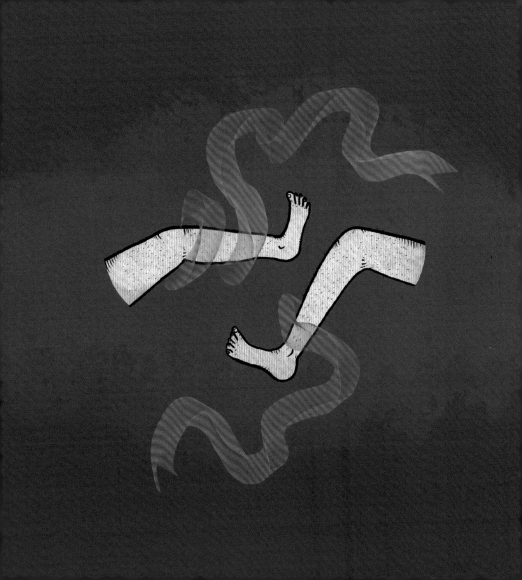

BACHELOR

You're safe with me, darling. I'll sit on you with my legs a-dangling. If a dubious fellow should approach, I will defend your honor by waving my little legs at him. If that doesn't terrify the bastard, he and I will leg-grapple, trying to trip each other while simultaneously binding each other's legs with silk.

Like a scene right out of *Fifty Shades of Three Stooges.*

I am a

SPIDER MITE

Tetranychus urticae

If you're wondering what *she's* doing while he's sitting on top of her, she's just being jailbait (second larval stage). Immobile, molting, and blissfully unaware, she will eventually emerge as wife material for the winning male.

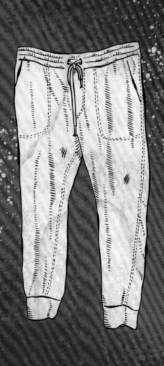

BACHELORETTE

When I'm not in the mood for sex, I don't make up excuses.
I just release a powerful dong-shrinking pheromone, the fragrance
equivalent of "no way in hell." It has notes of headache, sweatpants,
mother-in-law, and a lingering dry-down of *Murder, She Wrote*.
It's so effective, not only will you stop putting the moves on me;
you'll help me shop for throw pillows online.

I am a

BURYING BEETLE

Nicrophorus americanus

Before you get sulky, guys, the burying beetle is practically a nympho year-round, except for just three days after giving birth to *multiples*. So cut her some slack. The pheromone brilliantly suppresses her sex drive so that both the mother and the father will tend to the existing babies instead of trying to make new ones.

SALIVA

Spit, the bad boy of bodily fluids, is very gross and rude. But these guys don't agree. And before you get all judgy about it, just remember: kissing.

CAMEL

The mate-seeking male froths at the mouth until he looks like an Englishman at an Ibizan foam party. And that's not all: He fills his soft palate with air and lets it hang outside his mouth like an extra set of testicles.

SCORPION FLY

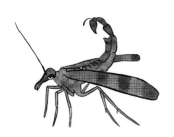

Females judge their mates entirely on salivary skills. The male's nuptial gift is a nutritious spitball that draws her in and keeps her from killing him.

REGENT BOWERBIRD

Leave it to these Dutch masters to put spit to elegant use. Males decorate their bowers with their own blue-green saliva "paint."

BACHELOR

I'm not a pervert, I swear. I'm just a guy with *really* shitty vision who's looking for The One. And honestly, you all look alike to me. Everyone I see is just a blurry, sexy possible wife. Just like on the first night of *The Bachelor*. Even your Dad. Even Aunt Phyllis. (Especially Aunt Phyllis.) I'm sorry I made everyone feel weird at Thanksgiving. It won't happen again, but it might.

I am a

DEEP-SEA SQUID

Octopoteuthis deletron

Two words for the deep-sea squid's mating style: swift and indiscriminate. It's dark as hell under water, and the only thing distinguishing a female from a male is a tiny patch of wrinkled skin—so a male can either spend precious hours finding the female in the room, or he can just slap a sperm packet on everything that moves.

BACHELORETTE

Will I date a man just because he has a great apartment? Yes. I'm
always looking for good properties. When I find one, I just lie
down and wave my legs outside the front door. It drives the guy
absolutely mad. He invites me to move in, like, instantly. And
then, God bless him, he moves out and leaves the whole place to
me. He seals me inside, but as long as I have internet, I'm good.

I am a

SAND-DWELLING WOLF SPIDER

Allocosa brasiliensis

In an unusual spiderly role reversal, the female seeks and pursues the male, as long as he has a nice, deep burrow to "donate" to her and her eggs. Don't worry; she likes being sealed inside, where she can safely incubate her wee spiderlings.

BACHELOR

Watch this! I can pee while doing a handstand! Uh-oh.

I am a

GIANT PANDA

Ailuropoda melanoleuca

Handstands are cool. So is peeing. The real trick isn't doing them together, but acting like you meant it to happen when you are blinded by your own steaming-hot urine. Male pandas upside-down pee on trees to get their scent high up, and smell as tall as possible to the females who come by later. (Key word: *later*.)

STICKS

A stick might seem like the lamest gift of all time, so why do some of nature's nicest bachelors offer them? Maybe they're doing a fable type of test to see if you like them for the right reasons.

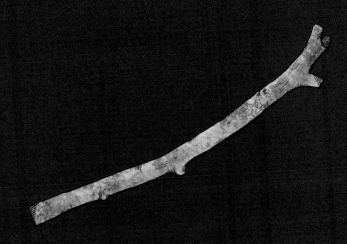

GREAT GREY SHRIKE

No basic carcass for you, m'lady. This gentleman hunts insects, reptiles, and small mammals, and kebabs them on sticks for his love interest.

RED VELVET MITE

This miniscule male arranges his sperm on small twigs—an icky little wonderland scientists call a "love garden." He then lays a silk trail to lure females to the spot.

SOUTHERN GROUND HORNBILL

If this guy offers you a stick, take it. It's his way of proposing, and he is a catch. He's strong and strapping, monogamous, an active co-parent, and his *eyelashes*—this drawing is not an exaggeration.

119

BACHELOR

All women just want to be protected. From spiders, mostly. So when you say you want a man with looks, integrity, blah blah blah, what I'm hearing you say is: *spider repellent*. If you mate with me, I will mist you in a bug spray so powerful that you *and* your future children will never have to worry.

P.S. Guess what. It works against bats, too.

I am a

SCARLET-BODIED WASP MOTH

Cosmosoma myrodora

On the eve of his nuptials, the male moth whips up his family recipe for spider repellent. (Don't want to give away any secrets, but it involves barfing on a poisonous dogfennel plant, soaking up the toxins, and storing them in his cute belly pouch.)

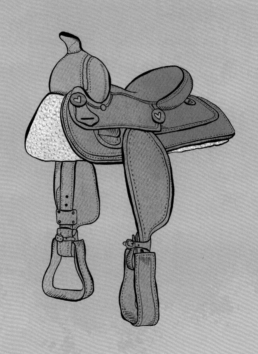

BACHELORETTE

My friends say I'm too nice, that I let guys take me for a ride. They're probably right. I literally do that. It's just that you guys are so vulnerable, and I feel kind of sorry for you. I'll end up giving you a piggy-back ride for like a week. And at some point you'll be like, "I'm so hungry; want to order pizza?" And I'll be like, "No, but I can secrete a delish wax from the back of my head." And so you'll just eat that the whole time, and you'll be fine.

I am a

ZEUS BUG

Phoreticovelia disparata

Scientists suggest that this arrangement provides the female with security. Umm, can we talk about what it gives the male? It's called *everything*—transportation, great company, good sex, a stable family life, and a 24/7 back-of-head buffet.

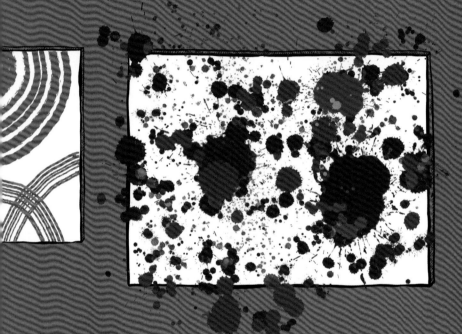

BACHELOR

I can poo and pee at the same time! But wait, there's more! Using a combination of my spinning tail and the most powerful farts on earth, I'll helicopter-spray my Winner's Blend far and wide. If you like what you see, just shower me with *your* dung!

I am a

HIPPO

Hippopotamus amphibius

While the bull goes full Jackson Pollock with his feces, the female's poop-back is more subtle. Scientists call this "submissive defecation." So now, apparently we ladies have to worry about whether our poo has confidence.

Love Language

FECES

Did you know that every day, you flush a valuable romantic resource down the toilet? Well, these turd-telligent animals are going to show you what you're wasting.

ROLLER DUNG BEETLE

The male rolls some poo into a gorgeous little truffle. If a female likes it, she hops on and goes for a ride. They eventually mate and raise their young on the dung ball. #dunglife

WHITE RHINO

Imagine—if you can—that Facebook is a huge, steaming pile of shit. The white rhino's social platform, a midden, is literally that: a communal dung-heap where they leave messages for each other.

WOMBAT

To mark territory and snag mates, the wombat actually shits bricks—darling little cubes that are perfect for making attracty-stacks.

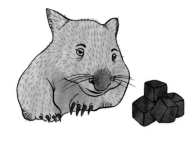

BACHELORETTE

If you like a woman who's large and in charge—like 200,000 times larger and in-charger than you—I'm the one. If you get close enough, I'll inhale you like a Tic Tac*, and turn you from a sexless little nothing into a very sexual, tiny little man! You'll get to spend the rest of your life inside my genital sac, producing sperm for me on demand. (Don't worry, you'll want to!)

* We've all done it by accident, but don't inhale Tic Tacs, kids.

I am a

GREEN SPOONWORM

Bonellia viridis

For green spoonworms, gender is all about who you know. The larvae have no predetermined gender. If you're a larva that spends enough time alone, you'll eventually become female. But if you brush up against a big mama, her green chemical coating will cause you to develop into a tiny male. From there it's just a quick suck up the proboscis, and a slide down into the "sac."

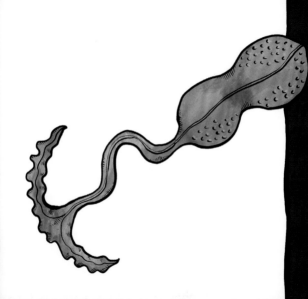

BACHELOR

I'm young, I'm fun, and my testes are disintegrating as we speak, so let's get this party started!!! My buddies and I are on a three-week devirginization rampage—we're talking fourteen-hour sex sessions with as many girls as we can find. Downside? Our bodies are literally falling apart. It's like Rumspringa with gangrene. You know those fast time-lapse films of an animal decaying? Basically, I'm that plus super horny.

I am a

MARSUPIAL MOUSE

Antechinus

All the females go into heat at the same time each year, setting off a mating frenzy. The sex and stress hormones cause total immune system collapse in the males. But they drag on until the very end, at which point even the most forgiving female might say "no, thanks." By the end of a fortnight, all the males are dead.

TOOTSIES

Guys. Do you ever wish there were a cuter, easier way to get laid? Without all that competitive aggression? Something funny to tell your kids someday? Sexual mimicry might be the method for you.

TOOTSIE

This determined "sneaker male" (Dustin Hoffman) pretends to be female to land an acting part on a major soap. He also lands the leading lady. And her dad. Best of all, he learns some important lessons about feminism.

JORDAN SALAMANDER

This little a-hole inserts himself between a couple mid-dance, rocks the female's part better than she does, then runs off with the guy's sperm packet *and* the girl.

CUTTLEFISH

This next-level impersonator is pure sitcom gold. He splits down the middle: male on the side facing the female love object, female on the side facing the male rivals.

RED-SIDED GARTER SNAKE

One of many males in a writhing sex ball around one "lucky" female, this sneaky snake emits a girly pheromone to distract and confuse the other males.

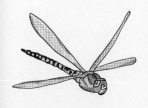

AND A YENTL...

Female dragonflies play this game, too. They mimic male coloration, apparently to avoid harassment. Or maybe they just want to study at the yeshiva!

BACHELORETTE

I can be aggressive toward men: kicking, hurling, possibly eating . . .
so if you want to make me less murdery during sex, you need to
give me a *really* good back massage. I mean a perfect, your-life-
is-on-the-line massage. I don't like Shiatsu. And use that massage
oil you used last time. One wrong move and you're so fucking
dead . . . . Oh, that's nice . . . lower, lower . . . ahhhh, better.

I am a

GOLDEN ORB-WEAVER SPIDER

Nephila pilipes

Males have evolved a brilliant massage technique called "mate binding" that involves a *strictly* choreographed back rub combined with a soothing silk wrap full of sexual hormones. This reduces cannibalism and, hence, increases romance.

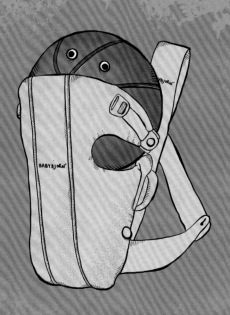

BACHELOR

Hey, there. I'm just a sexy, single dad out for a walk with my adorable man-raised baby strapped to my man-chest. How do I do it all on my own? Oh, it's a joy—but I get no sleep, ha ha ha!

What am I saying? You're gonna find out sooner or later. My baby is a basketball with googly eyes. I know women love single dads, so I borrowed my neighbor's Baby Björn, slam-dunked little Aiden in there, and he seems pretty happy!

I am a

THREE-SPINED STICKLEBACK

Gasterosteus aculeatus

Female sticklebacks prefer males who are good egg-daddies, so single males steal eggs from the nests of other males to use as mate-bait. Some have even evolved a structure on their dorsal fin that looks like eggs. Sneaky stickles!

BACHELORETTE

Warning: Do not read this if you have any fears.

This gets pretty dark for you, but hear me out, because it ends nicely for me. While we make love, I'm going to plunge my syringe-like proboscis into the top of your head, turn your innards into a smoothie, slurp you dry, and discard your empty husk. At this point, your ding-dong will probably break off (not that you'll care), but it will be totally intact, so that's nice, right?

I am a

MIDGE FLY

Serromyia

According to scientists, this fucking nightmare is "the best thing that could ever happen" to a bachelor midge fly, because it means his offspring will make it. Scientifically, there are probably better things that could happen to him, such as finding an authentic $1,000 bill on the sidewalk. Or just dying *any* other way.

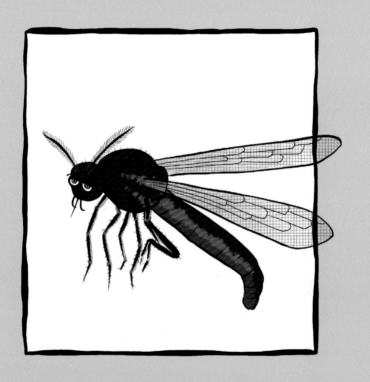

INDEX

Adélie penguin, 44
angler fish, 88
argonaut octopus, 40
balloon, 50–51
balloon fly, 51
banana slug, 64
bat, hammerhead, 71
bee, western honey, 48
beetle,
    burying, 102
    roller dung, 133
bird
    Adélie penguin, 44
    bowerbird, 82, 105
    canary, 95
    flamingo, 61
    frigatebird, 51

    great grey shrike, 119
    of paradise, 51
    parrot, 95
    prairie chicken, 61
    rock sparrow, 85
    southern ground hornbill, 119
bolas spider, 78
bowerbird,
    regent, 105
    satin, 82
burying beetle, 102
camel, 105
canary, 95
cannibalism, 32, 34–37, 94, 146, 154
capuchin monkey, 94
cement, 74
clownfish, 28

cottontail rabbit, 92

cricket, 68

cuttlefish, 143

dance, 58, 60–61

décor, 82, 84–85

deep-sea squid,108

dragonfly, 143

feces, 130, 132–133

field cricket, 68

fish

    angler fish, 88

    clownfish, 28

    cuttlefish, 143

    puffer fish, 85

    three-spined stickleback, 150

flamingo, 61

fly, 94

    balloon, 51

    parasitic, 68

    scorpion, 105

frigatebird, 51

frog, green, 71

gender, 28, 64, 136, 142–143

giant pacific octopus, 85

giant panda 116

gifts, 10, 50–51, 118–119

giraffe, 21

golden orb-weaver spider, 146

great grey shrike, 119

green frog, 71

green spoonworm, 136

hammerhead bat, 71

hermaphrodite, 28, 64

hippopotamus, 130

honey bee, western, 48

hooded seal, 51

humpback whale, 71

hyena, spotted, 14

Japanese macaque, 95

Jordan salamander, 142

lizard,

    New Mexico whiptail, 24

    tegu, 54

lobster, 21

macaque, 95

mantis, praying, 32, 94

marsupial mouse, 140

massage, 146

meerkat, 95

midge fly, 154

mimicry, sexual, 142–143

mite,

red velvet, 119

    spider, 98

monkey,

    Capuchin, 94

    Japanese macaque, 95

moth, 78, 122

mouse, 94

    marsupial, 140

necrophilia, 54

New Mexico whiptail lizard, 24

nursery web spider, 10

octopus,

    argonaut, 40

    giant pacific, 85

orangutan, 95

panda, giant, 116

parasitic fly, 68

parasitism, 68, 74, 88, 136

parrot, 95

pee, *see* urine

penguin Adélie, 44

poo, *see* feces

porcupine, 18

prairie chicken, 61

praying mantis, 32, 94

puffer fish, 85

rabbit, cottontail, 92

red velvet mite, 119

red-sided garter snake, 143

regent bowerbird, 105

rhino, white, 133

rock sparrow, 85

roller dung beetle, 133

saliva, 104–105

sand-dwelling wolf spider, 112

satin bowerbird, 82

scarlet-bodied wasp moth, 122

scent, 78, 102

scorpion, 61

scorpion fly, 105

sexual mimicry, 142–143

shiny jumping spider, 95

slug, banana, 64

song, 68, 70–71

southern ground hornbill, 119

spider mite, 98

spider,

    Australian red, 34–37

    bolas, 78

    golden orb-weaver, 146

    sand-dwelling wolf, 112

    shiny jumping, 95

spiny-headed worm, 74

spotted hyena, 14

squid, deep-sea, 108
sticks, 118–119
tegu lizard, 54
thanatosis, 10
three-spined stickleback, 150
Tootsie, 142
urine, 18, 20–21, 116
western honey bee, 48

whale, 70–71
white rhino, 133
wombat, 133
worm,
    green spoon, 136
    spiny-headed, 74
Yentl, 143
Zeus bug, 126